■ SCHOLASTIC

News

Nonfiction Readers

Pluto
Dwarf Planet

by
Christine Taylor-Butler

Children's Press
An Imprint of Scholastic Inc.
New York Toronto London Auckland Sydney
Mexico City New Delhi Hong Kong
Danbury, Connecticut

These content vocabulary word builders
are for grades 1–2.

Consultant: Michelle Yehling, Astronomy Education Consultant

The image on the cover is an artist's rendition of Pluto.

Photo Credits:

Photographs © 2008: DK Images: 4 top, 13; NASA: 11 (John Hopkins University Applied Physics Laboratory/ Southwest Research Institute), 23 bottom (A. Schaller/ ESA), cover, 5 top right and bottom right, 10; Photo Researchers, NY: 2, 5 top left (Chris Butler), 1, 4 bottom right, 7 (Lynette Cook), back cover, 19 (Lynette Cook/SPL), 23 top (Mark Garlick), 15 (NASA/ESA/STScI), 5 bottom left, 9 (Deltev van Ravenswaay).

Illustration Credits:

Illustration pages 20–21 by Greg Harris

Illustrations page 4, 17 by Pat Rasch

Book Design: Simonsays Design!
Book Production: The Design Lab

Library of Congress Cataloging-in-Publication Data
Taylor-Butler, Christine.
Pluto : dwarf planet / By Christine Taylor-Butler.—Updated ed.
    p. cm.—(Scholastic news nonfiction readers)
Includes bibliographical references and index.
ISBN-13: 978-0-531-14751-1 (lib.bdg.)   978-0-531-14766-5 (pbk.)
ISBN-10: 0-531-14751-7 (lib. bdg.)   0-531-14766-5 (pbk.)
1. Pluto (Dwarf planet)—Juvenile literature. I. Title.
QB701.T39 2008
523.48'2—dc22   2006102779

1 2 3 4 5 6 7 8 9 10 R 17 16 15 14 13 12 11 10 09 08

CONTENTS

Word Hunt 4–5

Pluto! 6–7

Dwarf Planets 8–9

Where Is Pluto? 10–11

What Is Pluto Made Of? 12–13

Pluto's Moons 14–15

Pluto's Orbit 16–19

Pluto in Our Solar System 20–21

Your New Words 22

Other Dwarf Planets 23

Index 24

Find Out More 24

Meet the Author 24

WORD HUNT

Look for these words as you read. They will be in **bold**.

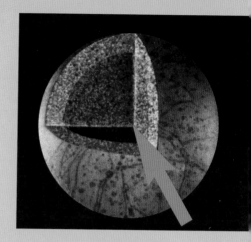

core
(kor)

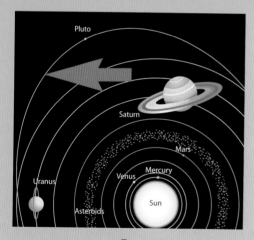

orbit
(**or**-bit)

Pluto
(**ploo**-toh)

4

moon
(moon)

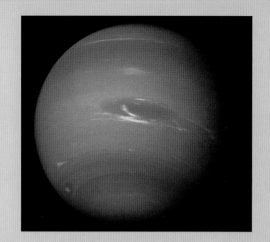

Neptune
(**nep**-toon)

solar system
(**soh**-lur **siss**-tuhm)

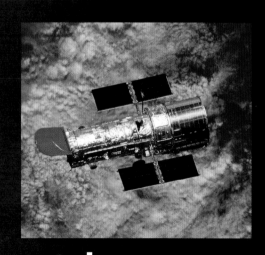

telescope
(**tel**-uh-skope)

Pluto!

Pluto is very far away.

Some pictures have been taken of Pluto. But in them, the surface of Pluto is hard to see.

Many pictures of Pluto are painted by artists.

An artist drew this picture of Pluto.

Pluto is a dwarf planet.

Dwarf planets are round like planets. But they are smaller. The space around them is full of smaller objects.

The area around planets is mostly empty.

Both planets and dwarf planets are found in the **solar system**.

Pluto

Sun

9

Scientists know that Pluto is made of both rock and ice.

The outside of Pluto is mostly solid ice.

The inside is called the **core**.

Scientists are not sure how much of the core is rock or ice.

core

13

Earth has one **moon**. Pluto has three.

They are called Charon, Hydra, and Nix.

Charon and Pluto look alike. They both look like icy balls, but Charon is smaller than Pluto.

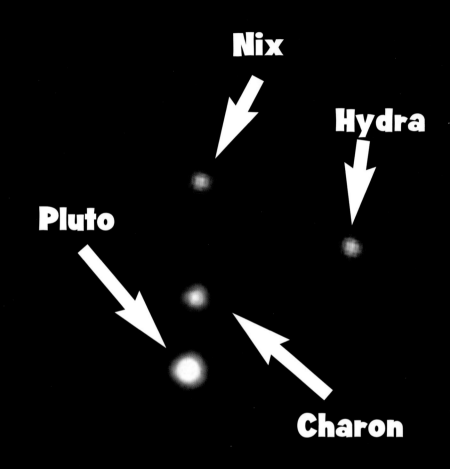

Nix

Hydra

Pluto

Charon

Charon is about half the
size of Pluto.

Pluto goes around the Sun on a path called an **orbit**.

Pluto's path is shaped more like an oval than most planets' orbits.

Sometimes Pluto's orbit crosses **Neptune's** orbit. But Pluto and Neptune will never hit each other.

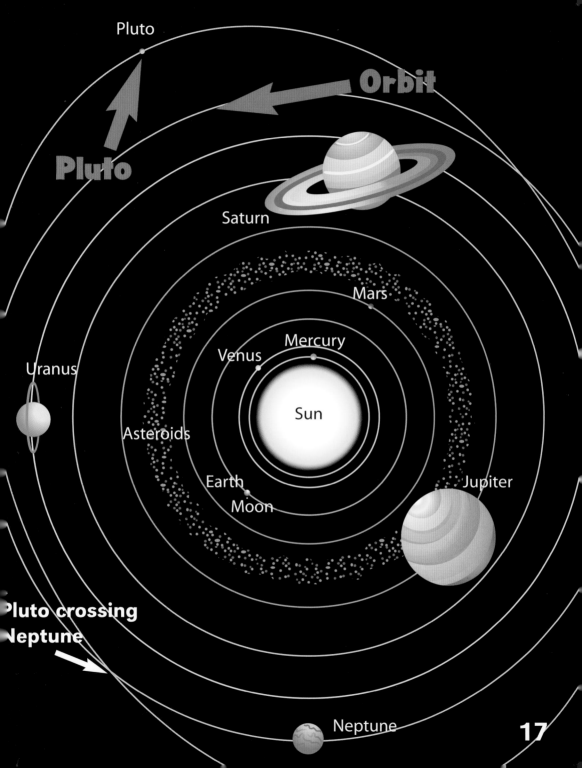

Pluto

Orbit

Pluto

Saturn

Mars

Venus

Mercury

Uranus

Sun

Asteroids

Earth

Moon

Jupiter

Pluto crossing
Neptune

Neptune

17

In 2226, Pluto will cross Neptune's orbit.

But Pluto will still be far away.

From the surface of Pluto, the Sun will still look as small as a star.

Will we know what Pluto really looks like by 2226?

Maybe!

Sun

Pluto

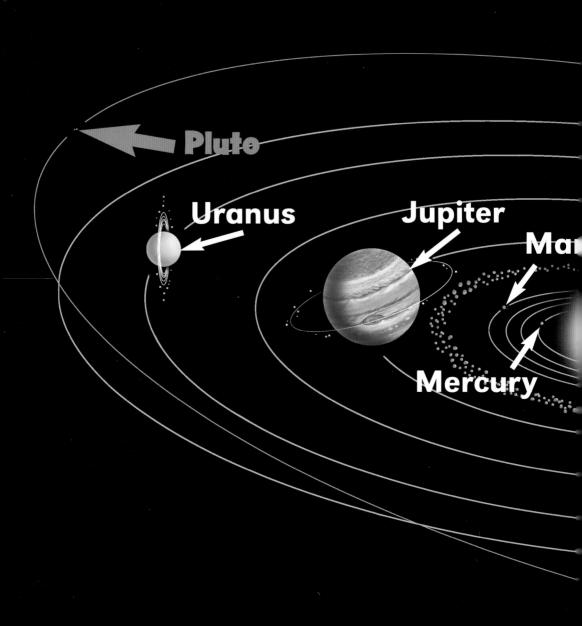

Pluto

Uranus

Jupiter

Ma[r]

Mercury

PLUTO

IN OUR SOLAR SYSTEM

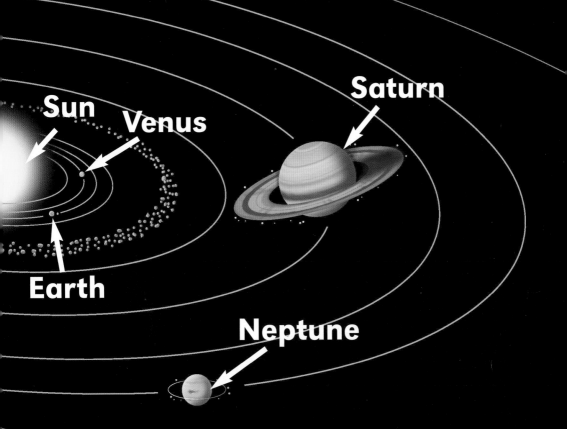

Sun

Venus

Saturn

Earth

Neptune

YOUR NEW WORDS

core (kor) the inside of an object

moon (moon) an object that circles a larger object

Neptune (**nep**-toon) a planet named after the Roman god of the sea

orbit (**or**-bit) the path an object takes around another object

Pluto (**ploo**-toh) a dwarf planet named after the Roman god of the underworld

solar system (**soh**-lur **siss**-tuhm) the group of planets, dwarf planets, moons, and other things that travel around the Sun

telescope (**tel**-uh-skope) a tool used to see things far away

Other Dwarf Planets

Ceres is found in an area
between Mars and Jupiter
called the Asteroid Belt.

Eris is in the Kuiper Belt, a
ring of icy rocks outside the
orbit of Neptune.

INDEX

Charon (moon), 14
core, 12

dwarf planets, 8

Hydra (moon), 14

ice, 12

moons, 14

Neptune, 16, 18
New Horizons space-
    ship, 10
Nix (moon), 14

orbit, 16, 18

pictures, 6
planets, 8, 16

rock, 12

size, 8, 14, 18
solar system, 8, 20–21
spaceships, 10
Sun, 10, 16, 18
surface, 6, 18

telescopes, 10

FIND OUT MORE

Book:

Burnham, Robert. *Children's Atlas of the Universe.* Pleasantville, NY: Reader's Digest Children's Publishing, Inc., 2000.

Web site:

Solar System Exploration
http://sse.jpl.nasa.gov/planets

MEET THE AUTHOR

Christine Taylor-Butler is the author of more than twenty books for children. She holds a degree in Engineering from M.I.T. She lives in Kansas City with her family, where they have a telescope for searching the skies.